Munchy

and

Jumpy Tales

VOLUME II

Kids Workbook with Social and Emotional Learning
Activities for Managing Anxiety, Calming Anger,
and Teaching Mindfulness

Stories and Games for Children Age 5 - 8

Written by Noah Teitelbaum
Illustrated by Julia Gootzeit & Marisa Randles

Published by Empowering Education
1001 Bannock St.
Denver, CO 80204
(720) 766-5765
www.empoweringeducation.org

Written by Noah Teitelbaum

Illustrated by Julia Gootzeit & Marisa Randles

Book Design & Layout by Kory Kirby

ISBN 978-1-7349393-2-3

Printed in the United States of America

Contents

Note to Adults

If you already read Munchy and Jumpy, Volume I, welcome back! I hope you and your little ones enjoy Volume II, in which you meet some new characters and read about some double-days that go wrong!

If you haven't met the bunny twins yet, in a couple of pages you'll meet Munchy and Jumpy as they learn to do *"double-days,"* repeats of a day gone bad. (Have you seen the movie *Groundhog Day*?) You can find the origin story on our website when you register this book. These stories are part of Empowering Education's Social and Emotional Learning program. They are designed to be read aloud to children, enjoyed, and then discussed. Each story highlights a social emotional skill, including mindfulness, which is the act of paying attention to what's going on inside and around us.

At points in the stories, you'll find optional suggestions for movement or discussion. Look for these:

> **Let's sniff like Munchy does.**

> **How do you think Jumpy is feeling?**

Pick and choose which ones to use, based on how engaged your listeners are, their age, etc. Too many interruptions can prevent kids from becoming absorbed with the story, but questions or movement can also help squirmier readers stay engaged and go deeper with their thinking.

If you want some additional resources that go along with these stories— including a bonus story!—or just to learn more about our program, which is available for K-8 schools, go to *empoweringeducation.org/book*

Let's go have some double-day adventures!

— Noah Teitelbaum, *Executive Director and Munchy and Jumpy fan*

I

An Allergy to You

If your students might not know what an allergy is, discuss.

A long time ago, but not too long ago, and far away, but not too far away, there lived twin rabbits, Munchy and Jumpy. They lived in a hole that was small, but not too small, in a tree that creaked loudly in the wind, but not too loudly.

One morning, Mother woke the twins and told them she would work in the garden all day. *"There's oatmeal on the stove for your breakfast,"* she said, as she headed outside.

The bunnies jumped from bed and started playing Rabbit Ring Toss. Munchy walked around waving his ears. When Jumpy's ring finally landed on his ear, Munchy's nose started twitching.

Let's try to make our noses twitch.

"*Something's burning!*" he cried. He ran to the stove and turned off the flame.

They looked into the pot at blackened oatmeal.

"*I'm pretty hungry,*" Munchy said.

"*You're always hungry,*" replied his sister. "*If Momma didn't put food high in the cupboard, you'd eat everything.*"

"*I would not!*" replied Munchy.

His sister laughed. "*You eat all the time! You're a pig. Look at your paw. You're holding a snack!*"

"*You're so rude!*" shouted Munchy. He turned his back and walked to a chair by the window.

Munchy didn't look at Jumpy, even when she invited him to chase cloud shadows outside. It was like he couldn't hear her at all.

Jumpy walked back and forth, wondering when Munchy would talk.

Let's walk back and forth, worrying about Munchy.

After six laps around the room, Jumpy couldn't take the waiting. "*Munchy, you are a stinky no-talking always-hungry little bunny!*" she yelled. "*You make me so mad! Don't sit there and pretend I'm not here!*"

"*You shouldn't be so rude!*" called Munchy. He returned to the window and pretended not to hear.

The day didn't get any better. As their empty bellies grumbled, the bunnies argued even more. By afternoon, the only thing they could agree on was doing the day over. They sat back-to-back in their room, closed their eyes, clenched their paws, and made their double-day wish.

Go ahead and close your eyes, squeeze your hands, and repeat after me.

"Double-day, double-day, make it a double-day."

"Double-day, double-day, let us try another way."

What do you think the bunnies will do differently this time?

The bunnies started to take three deep breaths as their Uncle had taught them to do.

Let's breathe with them.

One. Two.

Just then, a gust of wind blew through the window. It brought pollen dust from a flower that tickled the bunnies' noses. Instead of taking a third breath, they sneezed. Achoo! When they opened their eyes they were back in the morning. Though everything seemed a little more sparkly, their noses kept tickling. The oatmeal started to burn.

Just like last time, Munchy turned off the stove. Just like last time, they looked and saw burnt oatmeal. And just like last time, Munchy said, "*I'm pretty hungry.*"

Do you remember what Jumpy then said?

Just like last time, the bunnies started arguing, but every time they got to a certain word, they sneezed. "*Achoo!...always hungry,*" said Jumpy. "*If Momma didn't put food high in the cupboard, I bet…*" she sniffed and sneezed again. "*Achoo!… eat everything.*"

And just like last time, Munchy started to argue. But this time, he sneezed, too: "*Achoo so rude!*"

Later, Munchy sat by the window and pretended not to hear. Jumpy did six laps around the room and could take no more waiting. *"Munchy, Achoo! are a stinky no-talking always-hungry little bunny!"* Which she followed by saying, *"Achoo! make me so mad."*

The bunnies knew something was not right.

> **Why do you think the bunnies are sneezing?**

After a few more sneezes, the twins realized every time they tried to say *"you"* they sneezed, instead. The bunnies were still upset and wanted to say what had hurt their feelings. But since they couldn't say *"you"* without sneezing, they had to say things differently.

Munchy wanted to mention how Jumpy said something about eating too much. Since he couldn't say "*you*" without sneezing, he said, "*Munchy, I feel embarrassed when my eating is talked about.*"

When Jumpy wanted to say something about Munchy ignoring her, she found that—if she didn't want to sneeze—all she could talk about was her feelings. She said, "*I feel lonely and nervous when I don't get an answer.*"

With this way of talking, they didn't get as angry. Jumpy felt bad that she had said something about Munchy's eating. Munchy felt a bit sad that he'd ignored Jumpy and made her feel lonely and nervous.

Once the bunnies shared how they felt, the day got better. The bunnies went outside to chase cloud shadows and help Mother in the garden. They sneezed less as the day went on.

Later, Jumpy dug up the prettiest and sweetest carrot from the garden. She was about to take a bite when she looked at her brother, who watered the lettuce carefully, but not too carefully. She stood, jumped over to him, and handed him the carrot. "*I love you,*" she said, without sneezing.

The End

Discussion Questions:

1. Why did Munchy get upset?

2. Why did Jumpy get upset?

3. What word caused the allergic reaction?

4. When is it hardest to say how you're feeling?

5. Let's listen to the two ways that Jumpy talked to Munchy about being ignored:

   The first time she said *"You make me so mad. Don't just sit there and pretend I'm not here!"* The second time she said *"I feel lonely and nervous when I don't get an answer when I ask a question."*

   Which one would you rather hear? Why?

Activity:

Fill in the following I-Statements below:

I feel HAPPY when _____.

I feel SAD when _____.

I feel EXCITED when_____.

I feel ANGRY when _____.

I feel SCARED when _____.

I feel DISGUSTED when _____.

Play a game in which you don't use the word "*you*" in a conversation. For a Social and Emotional Learning challenge, role-play a conversation about a recent conflict.

> **For online resources and a bonus story, go to www.empoweringeducation.org/book**

Journal:

Draw a picture of your favorite part of the story you heard OR draw a picture of yourself telling someone how you feel.

Coloring Page:

2

A Wild Ride

A long time ago, but not too long ago, and far away, but not too far away, there lived twin rabbits, Munchy and Jumpy. They lived in a tree in a park that was quiet, but not too quiet, with many places to explore on a sunny day.

With big smiles, the bunnies planned a picnic.

They packed a basket with delicious-smelling food and a big, red and white blanket.

Out they went into the warm sunlight. They walked through the tall green grass and along the old stone wall. The bunnies stopped when they came to a field surrounded by bushes and a quiet, but not too quiet, stream. Jumpy spread the blanket while Munchy stared at the basket.

"Food is good, food is great, it's so good that I can't wait!" he sang. His sister banged on the bumpy blanket to smooth it.

Let's smooth out a blanket.

When they sat down for lunch, Munchy ate and ate. He ate a small carrot, half a cucumber, three slices of bread, another carrot, two strawberries, a sweet pea, one more carrot, and some corn.

Let's all pretend to eat a lot of food.

Munchy felt stuffed! His mother and sister had never seen him eat so much food. Pieces of food covered his shirt.

"*You don't look so good,*" said Jumpy. "*Are you okay?*"

Munchy tried to answer. Instead, he just burped, rolled over, and fell asleep. He soon snored loudly.

Let's all snore.

Mother and Jumpy decided to explore the field.

Underneath Munchy, a chipmunk named Charlie discovered his tunnels needed repairs. When Jumpy had banged the bumps to smooth the blanket, she had crushed Charlie's tunnels! As Charlie worked, a wonderful smell reached his nose. He smelled food!

> **What food do you remember Munchy ate?**

Charlie smelled bits and pieces of a small carrot, half a cucumber, three slices of bread, another carrot, two strawberries, a sweet pea, one more carrot, and some corn.

Charlie poked his head from a tunnel and saw Munchy on the blanket, snoring loudly. He saw pieces of food on Munchy's shirt. Bingo! Charlie crept up to Munchy, climbed on his chest, and bit a piece of cucumber. He turned around to eat a piece of strawberry, and his tail tickled Munchy's nose.

The tickles woke Munchy. When he opened his eyes, he saw a bushy tail.

"*What's that?!*" he cried, and his body tensed.

> **Let's all pretend to be scared and have our bodies tighten up.**

The way Munchy tensed made his chest move quickly. Charlie was tossed into the air.

Fortunately, Charlie landed back on Munchy's chest. Unfortunately, Munchy couldn't get him off. Munchy shook, but the chipmunk would not let go! Munchy spun in a circle, but Charlie still would not let go. Munchy spun, and Charlie held tight. Now dizzy, Munchy fell to the ground.

> *Try to get Charlie off your shirt like Munchy.*

Charlie still held on tight. Jumpy, returning from her stream-jumping adventure, noticed the chipmunk.

"*What a cute friend!*" she said.

"*Cute?*" said Munchy. "*He won't let go! I need to do a double-day to get him off me.*"

Jumpy looked confused. "*I don't think you need a double-day, Munchy. Try calming him down.*"

Munchy looked at Charlie and saw the chipmunk's muscles were tensed.

Let's tense our entire bodies, like Charlie.

Munchy realized the chipmunk was small and scared, and he wasn't dangerous at all. Jumpy was right—there was no need for a double-day. As Munchy slowed his breathing, his chest moved up and down. He could see Charlie's grip relax as the chipmunk moved up and down with his breath.

> **Let's lie down and put a breathing buddy (stuffed animal) on our chests and watch it go up and down.**

Charlie released one paw and smiled a little.

"*Okay, little guy, you can relax,*" Munchy said and gently lifted Charlie from his chest. "*Let me give you a better ride.*" He placed Charlie on his belly. Munchy breathed deeply into his belly. Charlie rose high into the air and then slowly came down.

> **Let's make our breathing buddies slowly go up high and then down low.**

Munchy breathed deeply and slowly. The chipmunk soon relaxed and so did Munchy. Charlie sat on different parts of Munchy's shirt to see how the ride was different.

> Let's try moving our breathing buddies around and see how it feels to move them up and down in those different places.

Before long, it was time to leave. As the bunnies folded their blanket, they realized Jumpy had banged Charlie's tunnels shut, so they helped him rebuild. When they finished, Charlie hugged each of the bunnies and ran back into his home.

From that day on, when Munchy wanted to relax, he remembered what it was like to have Charlie on his shirt. He would pretend to give him a ride and send him high into the air, but not too high.

The End

Discussion Questions:

1. What happened to Charlie's tunnels?

2. How did Munchy try to get Charlie off of him?

3. What calmed down Charlie and Munchy?

4. What was it like when your breathing buddy was on your chest? What about on your belly? Do you have a favorite place?

5. How does deep breathing make you feel?

6. When would you want to do that sort of breathing?

Activity:

Practice deep belly breaths. One option is to use a breathing buddy, as described in the story. Another kid-favorite is the *"starfish breath."* Raise one hand and spread out the fingers. With one finger of your other hand, trace up and down each finger of the raised hand. As you trace up a finger, breathe in. As you trace down a finger, breathe out. Breathe in as you go up the thumb, breathe out as you go down the thumb. Up the next finger in, down the finger out, up and in, down and out. Keep going and then come back the other way.

> **For online resources and a bonus story, go to www.empoweringeducation.org/book**

Journal:

Draw a picture of your favorite part of the story you heard OR draw a picture of yourself taking a deep breath with a breathing buddy.

Coloring Page:

3

Sticky Sticks

A long time ago, but not too long ago, and far away, but not too far away, there lived twin rabbits, Munchy and Jumpy. They lived in a hole in a tree with their mother, in a park that was wild, but not too wild, wandering far, but not too far.

"*Let's find logs and look at bugs underneath,*" said Jumpy, one bright fall day.

The twins found an old log half-buried in the dirt. They pushed, and a family of beetles appeared. "*Wow,*" Munchy said, "*so many!*"

Jumpy ran to the next log and started pushing. Underneath was a pair of excited snakes. The bunnies were scared at first, but the snakes turned out to be fun for playing jump rope.

After the bunnies turned over their fifth log, Munchy spotted a huge pile of sticks and mud near a pond. "*Wow, there must be a million bugs in that one!*" he said. "*Let's pull out some sticks and see what happens.*"

"*I don't know if that's a good idea,*" Jumpy said.

"*It's quick to pick a stick. Do not worry, it's not a trick!*" her brother said. He jumped onto the pile and pushed a big stick. "*Wow,*" he said, "*this stick is, well, sticky!*"

> **Let's push and pull on sticks like Munchy.**

Together they pushed and pulled until a stick flew. That kicked other sticks and mud into the air, knocking over Munchy and Jumpy.

The bunnies stood and heard crying. When they looked into the hole, they saw small balls of shaking fur. One furball with a long, flat tail turned and raised a fist at the bunnies.

"*It's a beaver,*" whispered Munchy.

"*¡Váyase!*" cried the beaver. "*You've ruined our dam!*" The beavers threw mud balls and hit Munchy in the nose!

> **Cover your head, the beavers are throwing mud balls!**

The bunnies jumped off the dam, ran into the woods, and hid.

"*I didn't know that was a beaver dam,*" said Munchy sadly.

"*This is terrible,*" said Jumpy. "*We ruined someone's home!*"

They decided right then to have a double-day. They closed their eyes and made tight fists with their paws.

Let's squeeze our fists tightly and repeat after them.

"*Double-day, double-day, make it a double-day. Double-day, double-day, let us try another way.*"

They took three deep breaths.

> **Let's breathe with them.**

One. Two. Three.

> **What do you think the bunnies will do differently this time?**

When they opened their eyes, they looked at the pile of sticks, and everything seemed a little more sparkly. Just like last time, Munchy wanted to pull out sticks to see bugs.

Just like last time, Munchy said, "*Wow, there must be a million bugs!*" But this time, Jumpy put her paw on his and said, "*Let's listen.*"

They closed their eyes, took another breath, and listened. At first, they could hear only the loud noises. They heard the birds chirp. They heard a squirrel chatter. As they continued listening, they heard the stream. When they listened even more closely, they heard the soft wind in the trees. Finally, they heard a very quiet noise. It came from the pile of sticks.

Let's listen like Munchy and Jumpy to the sounds in our room.

Munchy wanted to go over and investigate, but Jumpy stopped him. They sat a bit longer to listen. They heard singing! As the bunnies listened, they could hear the song, "*Cumpleaños feliz, cumpleaños feliz...*" Then they heard cheering. It was a party!

The bunnies repeated what they'd heard: "*Cumpleaños feliz,*" they called. The noise in the stick pile stopped, and a little beaver face appeared. "*Hola?*" the animal said.

"*Hola!*" Munchy said. "*We heard you singing happy birthday.*"

The beaver, named Benito, explained it was his father's birthday. He invited the bunnies to the party in their dam. They followed Benito through a hole in the pile of sticks. They met the beaver family and tried new, tasty foods.

The bunnies played new games, including *"come el palo,"* which was a race to chew through a stick. Munchy was fast but no match for the beavers. Jumpy showed the beavers how she could jump over the dam, and Benito taught them to make mud balls. They threw the balls into the air and watched them splat on the ground.

> **Let's throw a mud ball high into the air and watch it splat.**

The bunnies stayed all afternoon. When they got home, they told Mother about new friends, new foods, and the "*come el palo*" game. They told Mother a lot, but not too much. They didn't tell her how they listened carefully and how they heard the beavers singing quietly, but not too quietly, and how listening got them invited to a party. But you and I know!

The End

Discussion Questions:

1. Why was Munchy excited to turn over logs and pull out sticks?

2. Why did the bunnies want a double-day?

3. What was the same the second time they went through their day?

4. What was different the second time they went through their day?

5. What happened differently because the bunnies quietly listened?

6. If you were Munchy or Jumpy and could do the day over, a third time, is there anything you would do differently?

7. If you could have superhuman hearing, what do you think you would hear?

Activity:

Play a game in which one person describes a drawing or Lego structure and the other has to try to copy it without looking and just based on what is said. (Questions allowed.)

For online resources and a bonus story, go to www.empoweringeducation.org/book

Journal:

Draw a picture of your favorite part of the story you heard OR draw a picture of yourself listening carefully.

Coloring Page:

4

Raking and Thanking

A long time ago, but not too long ago, and far away, but not too far away, lived twin rabbits, Munchy and Jumpy. They lived in a cozy tree with their mother, who scrubbed their ears hard, but not too hard, and gave the bunnies chores that took a long time, but not too long.

The bunnies spent the morning harvesting vegetables from their garden. The sun shone, and the rich smell of dirt was in the air. Munchy carried a bucket of zucchini into their house. Jumpy sighed as she finished picking peas.

Let's pick peas and throw them into a bag.

"*I'm glad that's over!*" she said, flopping to the ground.

"*What do you mean?*" said Mother. "*You still have to rake the leaves.*"

"*Rake leaves?!*" Jumpy said, sitting up. "*We live in a park. There are leaves everywhere. They're called leaves so we should leave them.*"

Mother gave her a long, serious look.

"*I can think of 14,000 things I'd rather do than rake leaves,*" Jumpy mumbled. "*Number one, jumping. Number two, running. Number three, climbing...*"

"*You may hate the rake, but there's no escape! Now it's time to shake and bake!*" Munchy hopped past with another bucket of zucchini.

Let's balance a basket of zucchinis on our heads.

"*That doesn't make sense. I'm not shaking and baking. I'll just be raking and raking,*" Jumpy muttered, walking toward the rake.

"*You want some help?*" asked Munchy.

"*No. There's no point, I'll be raking until I'm an old rabbit,*" Jumpy snapped and started to rake. "*Number four, drawing.*" As Jumpy continued to list things she'd rather do, she dragged her feet on the ground.

> **Let's rake some leaves and look grumpy.**

"*This is the worst day ever,*" Jumpy thought. "*I hate gardening!*"

Later, Jumpy started her list again. "*Number five, solving puzzles. Number six, racing butterflies. Number seven—*" She opened her eyes wide and said, "*Number seven, do a double-day!*"

With that, she clenched a paw around the rake. She almost said the usual words to do the day over, but she was grumpy and said the words differently.

"*Double-day, double-day, make it a better day.*"

"*Double-day, double-day, let all this work go away!*"

What does she usually say?

What do you think will happen this time?

Jumpy hadn't thought those words would do anything, since they weren't what her Uncle had taught. But when she opened her eyes, to her surprise, everything seemed a little gray. There was no garden! She looked around. There was no rake! She saw what seemed like a mile of leaves covering the ground.

She looked for Munchy and Mother but didn't see anyone.

She crunched through the leaves to the front door. When Jumpy stepped inside, she gasped. Gone was the warm, crackling fire. There was no zucchini in the cold and empty corner. Jumpy shivered. *"Mother? Munchy?"* she called. All she heard was the blowing wind.

"What happened?" Jumpy thought.

> **How do you think Jumpy feels? Why?**

She was getting cold, and Jumpy felt her stomach growl. She crawled underneath the blankets and wished for Munchy's warm body nearby. A tear trickled down her fur. She closed her eyes, clenched her fists, and whispered, "*Double-day, double-day, make it a double-day. Double-day, double-day, let me try another way.*"

She took three deep breaths.

Let's breathe with her.

One. Two. Three.

Jumpy opened her eyes and saw the sun sparkling on the big garden. She felt her heart grow warm and full as she heard Munchy chant, *"You may hate the rake, but there is no escape! It's now time to shake and bake!"*

Jumpy hopped up and shouted with joy! She ran to her brother and gave him a hug. She saw Mother through the window and jumped into the house to hug her and smile at the warm, crackling fire.

Jumpy hopped back outside, smiled at the garden, and grabbed the rake. *"Wow,"* Munchy said. *"You really like raking!"*

"No," she replied. "*I don't like raking, but I love being alive! I can think of 14,000 things that I'm happy for. One, I have a mother and brother. Two, we have a warm fire in our house. Three...*"

Mother and Munchy laughed as Jumpy raked and danced at the same time.

Let's rake and dance!

Later, the twins ran inside and wrote Mother a letter about all the things they appreciated about her, and they hid it under a pan in the kitchen.

That evening, Mother found the note. Mother's eyes got watery, and she smiled at them for a long time. She hugged her bunnies tightly, but not too tightly, and they sat for a dinner of potato and carrot soup. It was warm and spicy, but not too spicy. It was just the way Jumpy liked it.

The End

Discussion Questions:

1. What was different about this story from the other Munchy and Jumpy stories?

2. Why did Jumpy say different double-day words this time?

3. What happened when Jumpy said different double-day words?

4. What happened after she said the double-day words a second time (and said them correctly)?

5. What do you think Jumpy learned during this story?

6. Do you ever feel like Jumpy felt when raking the leaves? When?

7. Did Jumpy's feelings about raking change?

8. What do you think the note to Mother said?

9. If Jumpy were to keep listing the things she's happy for (or *"grateful"* for), what do you think would be on her list?

Activity:

Create your own family or house gratitude journal or dinner conversation routine, and have everyone write down, draw, or say three things that you are grateful for every day for one week (or for as long as you want). *"One thing I am grateful for is _____, because _____."*

Example: *"One thing I am grateful for is my sister, because she has always been there for me when I needed her the most."*

For online resources and a bonus story, go to www.empoweringeducation.org/book

Journal:

Draw a picture of your favorite part of the story you heard OR draw a picture of what you are grateful for.

Coloring Page:

About the Authors

NOAH TEITELBAUM was a school teacher and teacher-trainer, and is now the Executive Director of Empowering Education. He lives in Denver with his two children, Lilly Mae and Jonah, who helped develop these stories.

JULIA GOOTZEIT is a cartoonist and illustrator living in North Carolina. She loves hanging out with her cats, and trying new recipes. You can find more of her work at juliagootzeit.com

MARISA RANDLES is a graphic designer and illustrator based in Mexico. She loves to art things up, cook plant-based meals, and spend time outdoors with her husband and two boys. She can be found at www.gypsy-jungle.com

Made in the USA
Coppell, TX
28 March 2025

47651038R00048